Mr Marksbury's
Careful Choice of Beds
Sue Boyle

Sue Boyle

Mr Marksbury's Careful Choice of Beds

Time & Tide Publishing
London EC1

Published by Time & Tide Publishing 2013
London EC1

© Sue Boyle 2013

ISBN-13:978-1491021880

A CIP catalogue record for this book
is available from the British Library.

timeandtidepublishing@gmail.com

for Ian Newblé

Upon Westminster Bridge

Earth has not anything to show more fair:
Dull would he be of soul who could pass by
A sight so touching in its majesty:
This City now doth like a garment wear
The beauty of the morning; silent, bare,
Ships, towers, domes, theatres, and temples lie
Open unto the fields, and to the sky;
All bright and glittering in the smokeless air.
Never did sun more beautifully steep
In his first splendour valley, rock, or hill;
Ne'er saw I, never felt, a calm so deep!
The river glideth at his own sweet will:
Dear God! the very houses seem asleep;
And all that mighty heart is lying still!

William Wordsworth

I used to have a list of things from my school buddies of what kind of art material they wanted. I'd go up to the West End of London and spend the whole day knocking stuff off.

Ronald Biggs, thief

I was 14 when I started modelling. At the end of that first day my mum said, If you want to do this, you're on your own because I'm not traipsing around London ever again like that. It's a nightmare.

Kate Moss, model

It was just a typical London flat, but it was in a great neighbourhood. It was across from the Playboy Club, diagonally. From one balcony you could read the time from Big Ben, and from the other balcony you could watch the bunnies go up and down.

Harry Nilsson, singer-songwriter

I don't know what London's coming to – the higher the buildings the lower the morals.

Noel Coward, playwright

contents

mr marksbury's
careful choice of beds

From the Camden Town house clearance specialists,
with their stuffed birds, hallstands, cracked majolica
and out of tune pianos −

from the flotsam and jetsam of other shipwrecked
lives following her divorce, my great aunt Irene
furnished her two rooms.

After he closed the shop for the evening, Mr Marksbury
would deliver her purchases, take a glass of port
and reminisce

about those days when totters
could harvest London with a horse and cart
and the pickings if you were sharp −

a nice bit of cranberry, in the better streets
an unchipped piece of genuine Lalique −
but would not cross the hall into Irene's bedroom

though he himself had supplied the figured walnut bed
because that would have been a sure way in his opinion
to lose an extremely good customer.

A shame, he would say quite often to his partner, Mr Paul,
that our friend on the hill has never remarried.
She has an eye for a pretty thing.

the happiness of mr paul

We like Mr Marksbury's shop.
The carved bear hallstand
Johannes Brahms is not for sale
nor the wax death mask
of the third Napoleon.

Mr Marksbury's aunt and uncle
were a Pearly King and Queen
with a lock-up in Whitechapel
and a horse, Madison,
who pulled the cart.
Their godson Cyril was made
up on his twenty-first birthday
to a Pearly Prince.

On Sunday evenings Mr Paul
opens one of the parlour pianos
and rehearses our club routines.
At nine o'clock precisely
Mr Marksbury brings Earl Grey tea.

Mr Paul's mother
launched him when he was five.
His costume was sailor suits
with colour-coded ribbons on the hats –
pink for the cheeky songs,
blue for the weepies.
For Whitechapel weddings,
he was always in demand.

Mr Paul has not played in public
since he moved in with Mr Marksbury.
I've hung up my pumps, he says.
You don't put yourself out for money
when you've found true love.

family photographs

This is me and this is Flavia my friend
the poledancer from Spearmint Rhino.
The red dragon belongs to Mr Li
who pays our friend Archangel a whole day's wages
to work the cylinder that puffs the breath.
Archangel feels safer being a fiery dragon
than in his fishnet tights and siren corset
upstairs in Gerrard Street.

The living statue in the mirror sunglasses
is our friend from Antigua, Virgil Christopher.
It takes an hour each morning to paint him blue
and an hour each evening to get him back to his skin.
The four of us share a flat in Dagenham.

Here we are on the boardwalk at Whitstable
with Archangel's rescue ferret, Michael Jackson.
The man with the walking stick is Virgil Christopher
in his Sunday clothes. When the wind gets up
Flavia puts Michael Jackson inside
her Prada jacket to keep warm. He never bites.
Archangel dressed like a man before he left Latvia.
It doesn't matter. We're Londoners now.
We've all come from somewhere else.

mr marksbury's
advice

If you are lucky in this life, Ada,
and continue to be a considerate
and sensitive young girl,
one day one of the few remaining angels
might materialise for a moment,
retract his astonishing white wings
and ask you to help him voice
the terrible yearning for human affection
which assails his heart.

You will long to respond
but, being a lonely and emotionally
a rather neglected young person
and shackled perhaps also
by what Mr Paul and I regard
as your over-strict upbringing,
you might be too timorous –
the affectionate word might stay
unuttered inside your mouth.

It might then be your sorrow
to watch your unique opportunity
to experience love fly on.
Outcomes in this life are so often
less kindly than your average fairytale
would have you think.
I have been fortunate in love, Ada.
Be courageous, said Mr Marksbury.

seize the day
or words to that effect

Why procrastinate, I said to him? What do we stand to gain if we delay? We might have been bashful, signed up together for a Path to Happiness ten week study course, or treated ourselves to a Nile cruise to consult the sphinx. I can just see us on the foredeck in the evening, each of us brooding separately about the peril of commitment after so many years of living on his own.

But the body clocks were ticking. I was not exactly in the first flush when I fell in with Mr Paul and given our beliefs we could hardly expect a second bite of the cherry on the other side. Besides, I'm a businessman. My accountant was bound to say that living in two places was not an allowable expense. We were men of the world. After a couple of weeks, there seemed no point in it.

So I said, Mr Paul, why don't we just quit the dithering and get one of those partnerships? We'll be quids in on taxi fares if we tie the knot and we'll also be able to raise some extra stock capital on your flat. And he said, those are my sentiments exactly, Mr M, I'm glad you spoke up. *Carpe diem*, or words to that effect.

Grab your opportunities this side of the pearlies is our view.

You never know what's going to happen next.

survival skills

It was one of those desert nights, said Mr Marksbury,
when your bones were afraid they might fracture
with the cold. Daniel had been walking all day;
he was exhausted; he had to sleep.

The thing to remember, Ada, is that a lion
is one of the *felidae*, a complicated creature
capable of higher reasoning who will often
have other things on his mind than simply food.

And the desert winter we are speaking about here
was by all accounts as cold as the Great Frost of 1683
when you could sink the length of a hot poker
into the ice at old London bridge and not strike water.

It was cold as a comet's tail and the sleeping man
presented himself as a welcome source
of life-saving warmth. A felid is too wise to waste
such a stroke of good fortune by killing and eating it.

Two endangered creatures prevented each other
from freezing to death in the desert that night
and in doing so, contrary each to their education,
they accustomed themelves to each other's smell.

This changed Daniel's understanding of the world
and (as things turned out) gave him the knowledge
he would need later in Babylon to save his life.
A useful lesson, said Mr Marksbury.

a day out in dorchester
henry duke's auction house

a pair of leg irons
dredged from the River Thames
near the Tower of London
a theatrical crown and a collection
of theatrical hats and shoes
a bush baby and a golden breasted starling
a waxwork of George Bernard Shaw
wearing a tweed jacket and plus fours
a pair of entwined fighting snakes
two further snakes and a small frog
an iron shame mask with ass's ears and a candle
a waxwork of Queen Victoria automated
with a heaving chest and tapping foot
a german *pickelhaube* leather helmet
an african elephant
a boa constrictor
a red fox

a gilt-finished swan
a junior ringmaster's outfit
a waxwork of a child sticking out her tongue
a collection of simulated leather and cardboard hatboxes
a collection of framed music hall programmes
including Wilfred Pickles in 'Hobson's Choice'
at the Grand Theatre, Blackpool and others similar
a baby rhinoceros
a wrought iron mantrap
a half-length waxwork of a torso
with a knife plunged into his chest
a french executioner's axe

How it passes, they whisper
between the lots. Gloria mundi.
The glory of the world.

cloning the unicorn
Lot 376: a unicorn (monoceros unicornis)
For sale without reserve

White pony skin, an armature stuffed with straw,
a narwhal horn, a sorrow of mismatched eyes –
it was one of Professor Copperthwaite's Stuffed Curiosities
along with Thomas Bessie, the Famous Flying Cat
and Bruno, Queen Victoria's Boxing Bear.
Experts said the lodged *monoceros*
would fetch three thousand pounds.

Then began a perilous time for unguarded live white ponies.
Every giant fair had its Copperthwaite unicorn within the year.
Judging how many the market could take without suspicion –
the money went to the dealers who managed that.

breaking up the books

This graceful young woman
has been given Arts Council funds
to deconstruct books in public places
with the aim of encouraging
shoppers and tourists to re-engage
with the phenomenon of the printed word.

To break up an antique book,
you sever the spinal cord with a scalpel;
guillotine each folded page;
abstract what is commercially viable
then stack the remainder for the fire.
It is not for the faint-hearted.
True book breaking is a rough trade.

dolls
at the newark fair

The under-age Irish girls
in arm-linked cohorts flaunt around the fair –
cheeky, short-skirted, high-heeled, painted up,
flowers and fancy combs in their long thick hair.

By gaslight in palatial caravans
their fathers, uncles, brothers split the take
and oversee their sisters', daughters',
nieces' virgin sleep.

In the night pavilions, dolls,
with their halcyon absence of genitalia,
wait for the dawn collectors.
Strong men patrol the fierce perimeter.

moving on
for dave

Bubbled, tissued, boxed, the stock is snug.
The tailgates of trucks and transits are greedy tongues.
The black night hungers.
Towns and cities wait to reclaim their own.
Snow is a blessing: each flake is a little kiss.
The motorway unspools like new music.
Inky landscape turns into a song.

the out-of-town dealer
tries to sell a painting
to mr marksbury

What I want to say to her is,
this reaching out to the barely expressible,
this hunger to find words on the very edge,
this gnomic utterance –

I have to sell these things.

But his use of shadow, she explains,
that otherworldliness which manages to suggest
in the rich, apparently living moment
the countervailing possibility of death –

He paints too small for the money,
I hear me say. For that sort of money
people want real statement in a room.

But modesty was his statement, she explains,
the near-to-hand subject,
the least 'arranged',
the essential 'is' of things –

This is a painting of lilac.
My customers believe
that lilac is unlucky inside a house.

Lilac is out, I said.

monsieur loti's cat
has the chance to go travelling

What a comedian, what a dandy
this Monsieur Pierre Loti –
he had my round red cushion
made expressly to match his hat.

He used to leave me behind
when he went on his adventures
but now it is my turn to see the world
and where I go, he has to go –
Jerusalem, Paris, London, Washington –
he no longer has the choice.

And everywhere they ask the same questions:
who is that odd-looking, self-important man?
what on earth is he doing in that wonderful picture?
can anyone remember what was he famous for?

Monsieur Pierre wanted to be remembered
for his literary achievements
but I don't need to be remembered
because here I am.
It is enough achievement for me
just to be myself
on my ridiculous round red cushion
the ultimate full-frontally famous cat.

Monsieur Rousseau made a very good job of me –
you could run your fingers through my belly-fur
if they would let you. They won't.
We are insured for ten million euros.
Even my lovely white ears are out of bounds.

a portrait of cosimo

What is it, to narrow your eyes
like that against the sun
and a hawk drop down like that
to your outstretched hand
whether she will or not?

What is it to whistle
your hunting hound
and read in those helpless
eyes and hang of head
what fealty is
and what is servitude?

What is to to ride so high
on a horse, thigh
to flank, knee to shoulder,
rein to mouth one music,
melded like lovers,
running in the wind
whether horse will or not?

What is it, like this,
without adornment, all in black
to deal another's death,
to be without conscience,
to be without ill dreams?

It is to be me.
It is to be a prince.

Cosimo de Medici 1519–1574
Grand Duke of Tuscany

border control

So what was friendship?
said the angel at the gate.

A wild creature, I answered,
that chose to share
the shelter of my house.

When I was lonely after that,
I was not alone.

When I was negligent,
it did not take offence.

Each day it reminded me
there was no hurry;
we were not lovers;

we had all the time
that remained to us
in that world.

Outsiders thought it
unremarkable.

It had no idea
of before or afterwards.

It was manna, sometimes,
in the wilderness.

It was never a burden.

The gate is open, the angel said.

bereft

When I was young, I lived with a lion cub
above the pine shop at World's End. I was never
more dearly companioned than I was by him.

His purr enveloped you. Resting, his gaze withdrew
as if to say, this space, these moments with you,
whatever is coming next, they are enough.

That painting by George Stubbs in Manchester –
the Duke of Cumberland's cheetah much too shocked
by an antlered English stag to display his skills –

that bewildered creature with his anxious attendants,
his crimson belt, his crimson hunting cap –
surely though a captive he was loved?

These images haunt me – kings with their leopards,
Cosimo on his horse, the Duchess Anne with her pet
marmoset, the Doctor with Hodge his cat.

restored

One day they will make him marvellous again
the chariot horse whose fragments of statue
wait under this garden laid for a prince.

This oak tree will fall; its tangle of roots reveal
a sculptured eye, the arc of a hoof, the swell
of a polished haunch. It happens here in Rome.

They will replace his armature and speculate,
was this that dangerous tempered horse,
the stallion from the western provinces

who chafed and pawed the sand at the starting gate,
whose nostrils flared so wide at each tight turn
he delighted all of Rome? That legend of a horse

who grazes now
the night-blue meadows of Elysium
and waits for a kindly groom

to bring news that their sorrow is finished;
they can leave the ignoble city;
at last they are going home.

Farnese Gardens, Rome

the little street of the goose
venice 1849

So easy to exploit their weaknesses
these titled strangers, ignorant young men
craving a light they cannot see.

We have the skills, the wit, the varnishes
to cut and reconfigure any canvas
smuggled to our house.

We fray the linen, rub in pumice dust,
fret new gilding with a pouch of sand
and bury the stretcher nails to bring on rust.

A Bacchus, a dog, a saint – we can sell them all
providing the *craquelure* convinces
and the price is right.

The strangers believe they have purchased taste,
puff up like marsh frogs as they oversee
their trinkets into crates for the journey home.

We hear that fog inhabits the plain houses
where they boast that they outwitted us on price,
order fresh colours for the sombre rooms

to show off their new things.
As if it could be bought,
what we have.

Look at our lagoon, *signori.*
Luce sull'acqua. The light of heaven,
reflected on the water.

portraits at montacute

From the long gallery they look down on us,
two friends who had believed each other lost

and at four o'clock are still strolling
the green ride with so much to be said.

The volunteers are putting the house to bed
linen, lavender, beeswax, muslin shroud

because moth, dust and miasma do corrupt
as sorrow does, so many being gone.

Sun flares a candle on each window pane.
I would like to have made the trip to Lucca,

Matthew says, but no invitation came.
I think it might be time to give up the car.

If we had met up this morning, Matthew says,
we could have climbed Ham Hill.

From the tall windows, they look down on us –
Burghley, Essex, Monmouth, Dorchester,

the heirs, the hopeful daughters, the good wives,
the sycophants, the terrified, the vain –

and from the safe havens of their gilded frames
they note how slow we walk,

how well we suit the autumn metaphor –
our light on the ebb, our winter on its way.

time & tide

one

My favourite place, the terrace at Rotherhithe.
I watched the new glass city going up –
the banks, the fancy restaurants, the hotels –
and I asked myself
what will we look like down here
from one of those shiny towers?
Queer thing to be so far from the river,
like living in another world.

two

The Alma in Princelet Street. The Seven Stars.
The Frying Pan. The Crown and Dolphin.
On Stepney Green, The Ship. The Laurel Tree.
The Anchor and Hope at 90 Duckett Street
and The Knave of Clubs. All gone.
All gone into the dark.

three

Now may all lovers be as one
In bed and board, in hearth and home
And what is done be not undone.
Ding, dong, bell.

It don't take much to take a life
An evil heart, a butcher's knife
Now there are four, once there were five.
Ding, dong, bell.

Two queens were wearing cloth of gold
With pearls their velvet cloaks were sewn
For one the block, the other the throne.
Ding, dong, bell.

The drowned man drifts past Bermondsey
Through Blackwall Reach to Tilbury
The ebb will carry him to the North Sea.
Ding, dong, bell.

four

That's our Marie got up for the halls.
She's for the light but the five of us
are for the bloody dark.
Mary Ann Nichols. Annie Chapman.
Elizabeth Stride. Catherine Eddowes.
Mary Jane Kelly. You can walk
our murders any evening at seven
from Aldgate East. They'll have eight
pounds off you. You can pay on the night
or you can book ahead
with a credit card online.
It was the darkness did for us.
Sing for us, Marie.
Give us our eyes.
Undo the bloody dark.

five

In Spital Square, outside Carluccio's,
the girl from Poland is feeding biscuit crumbs
to her little dog and the Chechen boy
is breaking hearts with his accordion
while towers rise from the rubble of little streets.
Bucks Row. Dorset Street. Berners Street.
All gone. We are drinking *prosecco*.
It is hot, you complain, so hot.

a window
on cadogan square

The customary hour had reached its end.
Handshakes were offered. Farewells
were exchanged. I had imagined
we would meet again – unfinished talk,
ideas half touched upon.

But there is a last
time for everything, dear friend,
said Mr Marksbury, at least for those of us
who experience ourselves, rightly or wrongly,
as travellers through a time-limited universe.

A day begins like any other day –
a person waves from a platform
at a lover already encased
in a moving train.
The moment cannot return.

He brought me such good things –
my *escritoire*, my *boule*, my cranberry.
Mr Marksbury knows his glass.
This vase for instance:
flying curlews in side view, bas-relief
on a pattern of fish-scale cloud.
Dark green glass with milk-white patina.
1931 *Lalique*.

Of all the pieces he found me,
this will always be my favourite.

the unicorn
goes back to kew

The morning launch from Richmond whooped its horn;
the passengers crowded the guardrail in disbelief.
Their cameras would retain no images
of what they knew had surged upstream that day –
Thames cruise boat 'Cockney Sparrow'
with a unicorn on the triangle of deck above the prow.

The herons on Oliver's Island would remember
the unicorn passing; so would the woman
who had to haul the iron gate;
the child in the pushchair;
the wistful cross-bred dog.
Even the most secular were convinced
by what seemed to them not a new
but a deeply remembered grace
as the white creature chose the path
between the orangery tearoom
and the fantastic glasshouses.

Il sfiorare del silenzio. The passing of a silence
is what they call such transits in Italy
where they have a better understanding
of these things. Don't look for reasons, Ada.
Simply, that's how it was.
Something rare and gentle left our world
and will not return. We will not forget
what we have seen. We have each other,
said Mr Marksbury.

acknowledgements

I am very grateful to the editors of *Acumen* and *The North* in which two of these poems first appeared and to Smith/Doorstop for publishing the opening poem 'Mr Marksbury's Careful Choice of Beds' in *Too Late for the Love Hotel* which was one of the prize-winners in *The North's* 2010 pamphlet competition judged by the Poet Laureate Sir Andrew Motion.

I am also very grateful to Cafe poets Claire Coleman, Claire Dyer, Ray Fussell, Caroline Heaton, Jill Sharp and Susan Utting for including four of these poems in the sequence *Scenes from the Picture Trade* which they created and performed in the Oak Room at the Swan Hotel in Wells as part of the Bath Poetry Cafe's contribution to the Day of Poetry at the 2012 Wells Festival of Literature.

As for the dealers, auctioneers, restorers, customers and competitors who taught me so much and made my years in the antiques trade so alluring – they are far too many to name individually and far too fascinating and vivid ever to forget. Bath, Oxford, London, Penzance, Newark, Exeter, Shepton Mallet, Ardingly, Honiton, Bristol, Crewkerne, Newbury, Lille, Warminster, Hungerford, Topsham, Marlborough, Gloucester, Cheltenham, Paris, Wells, Birmingham, Bournemouth, Taunton, Frome – the trade is indestructible. As with all good memories, you have only to turn a stone to start a wing.

Sue Boyle

L'amore. La morte. How close they are.
The confusion of signs. The fiction of surfaces.

Sue Boyle's *Too Late for the Love Hotel* was a prizewinner in *The North*'s 2010 pamphlet competition judged by the Poet Laureate Sir Andrew Motion who said that the collection stood out for 'the attention the poems pay to their subjects' and 'the range and strangeness of its interests.' In *On Board Arcadia* the lover of the Emperor Hadrian tells his story alongside the piano-playing partner of a Camden Town house clearance dealer; Cosimo Duke of Tuscany shares space with Henri Rousseau's talking cat. An eighteenth century mother grieves for her ruined daughter to William Hogarth while the goddess Demeter looks for her own lost daughter in a Christmas Market in contemporary Rome.

Sue Boyle likes her characters to step out of history, darkness and silence and confide the core truths about their lives without the author getting in the way. Trained to teach drama and creative writing, she writes direct and accessible poems for the voice – or rather for the many voices in the series of short volumes which make up *On Board Arcadia*. A Londoner by family and background, she has lived in ten English counties and worked as a teacher, social worker, antiquarian print dealer, market trader in bric-a-brac and maker of hand-finished picture frames. For the past six years she has organised the Bath Poetry Cafe and the associated Cafe Writing Days.

Arcadia is a world full of surprise and revelation as the poems explore what lies below the surface of the ordinary and bring old histories into the present day. 'Sue Boyle's is the voice of a true original: her work has a wit and inventiveness all too rare in poetry today.' (Rosie Bailey)

On Board Arcadia

*A series of six themed short volumes
available at readings and workshops
or direct from Amazon.*

Volume One
A Day Out on the Thames
Twenty-two poems

Against a background of momentous historical events – the fires of the London blitz, the dropping of the atom bomb, the terrors of the Cold War – the poems in *A Day Out on the Thames* focus their affectionate attention on the aspirations and disappointments of one London family: the texture of treasured moments, daily life and familiar places, the complex of memories which becomes the inheritance of those who are left behind. There are sorrows, difficulty, loneliness, and loss, but it is the passion for living and for the wonder of life which the poems celebrate. The collection closes with the serenity of the prize-winning sonnet, 'Thinking About the Swans.'

*October 2013
ISBN-13:978-1483961668*

Volume Two
Mr Marksbury's Careful Choice of Beds
Twenty-two poems

Mr Marksbury's Careful Choice of Beds is a book about London, but not perhaps the London the tourist knows. One by one, strange characters make their intriguing cameo appearances: Virgil Christopher the living statue; Flavia the poledancer; the lonely collector of vintage glass. We visit a country auction and overnight at a giant antiques fair. We also meet a rescue ferret, a unicorn, a couple of angels and a famous talking cat. From Kew Gardens to Canary Wharf, Camden Town antiques dealer Mr Marksbury makes his way through this offbeat geography, shedding light on dark places and offering his idiosyncratic views on leading the good life. There are also useful lessons on how to fake an old master painting, lie down safely with a lion and recognise true love.

*October 2013
ISBN-13:978-1491021880*

Volume Three
A Respectable Neighbourhood
Thirty-nine poems

Behind the closed doors of houses, the closed doors of the heart – the secrets, dangers, delights and sorrows of human love. From first encounters to bereavement, with lovers ranging back from the contemporary to the depths of ancient myth, the collection takes its theme from 'A Leisure Centre is Also a Temple of Learning' and explores 'what happens next.' Will we be faithful, unfaithful, cherished, abandoned, blameworthy, innocent? We never know what waits behind the door until we make the frightening commitment to step inside the house of love.

October 2013
ISBN-13: 978-1490946917

Volume Four
Report from the Judenplatz
Nine Lamentations & A Play for Witnesses

The sequence of nine lamentations in *Report from the Judenplatz* is also presented as a play for witnesses to be shared by any number of participants as a way of honouring the victims of the Holocaust. Between 1939 and 1945 most of Europe turned its back on its Jewish citizens. This book tries to hear the voice of those absences – the abiding silence of the streets and squares emptied by the deportations – and to make a space in which to remember the richness of the culture which the Nazi genocide intended to destroy. The cover design is by kind permission of the Yad Vashem Holocaust Memorial and Institute in Jerusalem and profits from the sale of *Report from the Judenplatz* will be donated to the Yad Vashem UK Foundation.

October 2013
ISBN-13:978-1482776294

Volume Five
Ark Music
Twenty-six poems

Ark Music, the fifth volume of *On Board Arcadia*, is a strange, dark collection which explores the belief that man is the intended master of the earth. From the first lobe-finned fish to the last extinction, from the Trojan War to the threat of nuclear armageddon, we are casualties of our species' ambition and belligerence. A grieving celebration of the wonder and beauty of the planet as it turns in its 'cage of stars', the poems in *Ark Music* reach towards a gentler way of being in the world and try to open up a place in imagination for a new 'ark' so that what is left of the precious, varied and fragile might be better cherished and perhaps be saved.

October 2013
ISBN-13:978-1491041772

coming soon

Volume Six
A Small Menagerie

Time & Tide Publishing
London EC1

Made in the USA
Charleston, SC
08 October 2013